CALICO
BIRTHDAY BOOK

Illustrations by Penny Brown

A Sterling/Museum Quilts Book
Sterling Publishing Co., Inc. New York

JANUARY

JANUARY

1 _____

2 _____

3 _____

4 _____

5 _____

JANUARY

_____ 6

_____ 7

_____ 8

_____ 9

_____ 10

JANUARY

11 _____

12 _____

13 _____

14 _____

15 _____

JANUARY

_____ 16

_____ 17

_____ 18

_____ 19

_____ 20

JANUARY

21 _____

22 _____

23 _____

24 _____

25 _____

JANUARY

_____ 26

_____ 27

_____ 28

_____ 29

_____ 30

_____ 31

FEBRUARY

FEBRUARY

1

_____

2

_____

3

_____

4

_____

5

_____

6

_____

FEBRUARY

7 _____

8 _____

9 _____

10 _____

11 _____

12 _____

FEBRUARY

13

14

15

16

17

18

FEBRUARY

19 _____

20 _____

21 _____

22 _____

23 _____

24 _____

FEBRUARY

_____ 25

_____ 26

_____ 27

_____ 28

_____ 29

MARCH

MARCH

1 _____

2 _____

3 _____

4 _____

5 _____

MARCH

_____ 6

_____ 7

_____ 8

_____ 9

_____ 10

MARCH

11 _____

12 _____

13 _____

14 _____

15 _____

MARCH

_____ 16

_____ 17

_____ 18

_____ 19

_____ 20

MARCH

21 _____

22 _____

23 _____

24 _____

25 _____

MARCH

_____ 26

_____ 27

_____ 28

_____ 29

_____ 30

_____ 31

APRIL

APRIL

1 _____

2 _____

3 _____

4 _____

5 _____

APRIL

6

7

8

9

10

APRIL

11 _____

12 _____

13 _____

14 _____

15 _____

APRIL

_____ 16

_____ 17

_____ 18

_____ 19

_____ 20

APRIL

21 _____

22 _____

23 _____

24 _____

25 _____

APRIL

_____ 26

_____ 27

_____ 28

_____ 29

_____ 30

MAY

MAY

1 _____

2 _____

3 _____

4 _____

5 _____

MAY

6

7

8

9

10

MAY

11 _____

12 _____

13 _____

14 _____

15 _____

MAY

_____ 16

_____ 17

_____ 18

_____ 19

_____ 20

MAY

21 _____

22 _____

23 _____

24 _____

25 _____

MAY

26

27

28

29

30

31

JUNE

JUNE

1 _____

2 _____

3 _____

4 _____

5 _____

JUNE

_____ 6

_____ 7

_____ 8

_____ 9

_____ 10

JUNE

11 _____

12 _____

13 _____

14 _____

15 _____

JUNE

16

17

18

19

20

JUNE

21 _____

22 _____

23 _____

24 _____

25 _____

JUNE

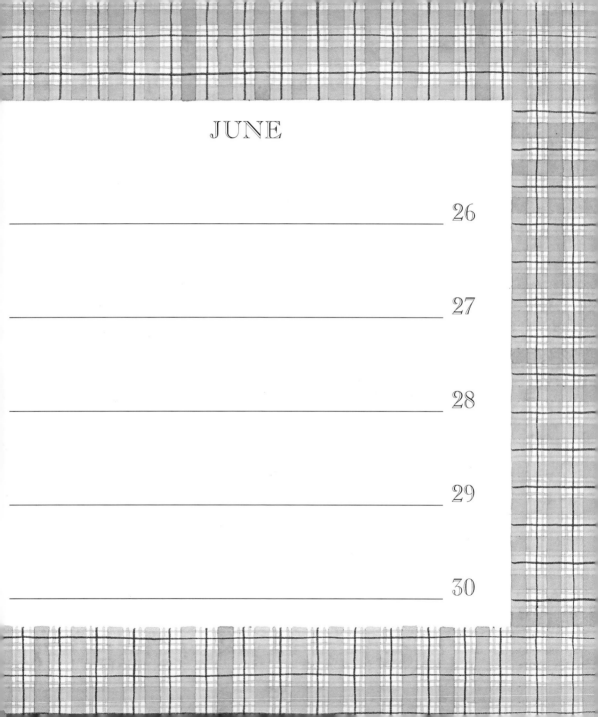

26

_____

27

_____

28

_____

29

_____

30

_____

JULY

JULY

1 _____

2 _____

3 _____

4 _____

5 _____

JULY

6

7

8

9

10

JULY

11 _____

12 _____

13 _____

14 _____

15 _____

JULY

_____ 16

_____ 17

_____ 18

_____ 19

_____ 20

JULY

21 _____

22 _____

23 _____

24 _____

25 _____

JULY

26

27

28

29

30

31

AUGUST

AUGUST

1 _____

2 _____

3 _____

4 _____

5 _____

AUGUST

_____ 6

_____ 7

_____ 8

_____ 9

_____ 10

AUGUST

11 _____

12 _____

13 _____

14 _____

15 _____

AUGUST

_____ 16

_____ 17

_____ 18

_____ 19

_____ 20

AUGUST

21 _____

22 _____

23 _____

24 _____

25 _____

AUGUST

26

_____

27

_____

28

_____

29

_____

30

_____

31

_____

SEPTEMBER

SEPTEMBER

1 _____

2 _____

3 _____

4 _____

5 _____

SEPTEMBER

_____ 6

_____ 7

_____ 8

_____ 9

_____ 10

SEPTEMBER

11 _____

12 _____

13 _____

14 _____

15 _____

SEPTEMBER

_____ 16

_____ 17

_____ 18

_____ 19

_____ 20

SEPTEMBER

21 _____

22 _____

23 _____

24 _____

25 _____

SEPTEMBER

_____ 26

_____ 27

_____ 28

_____ 29

_____ 30

OCTOBER

OCTOBER

1 _____

2 _____

3 _____

4 _____

5 _____

OCTOBER

_____ 6

_____ 7

_____ 8

_____ 9

_____ 10

OCTOBER

11 _____

12 _____

13 _____

14 _____

15 _____

OCTOBER

_____ 16

_____ 17

_____ 18

_____ 19

_____ 20

OCTOBER

21 _____

22 _____

23 _____

24 _____

25 _____

OCTOBER

_____ 26

_____ 27

_____ 28

_____ 29

_____ 30

_____ 31

NOVEMBER

NOVEMBER

1 _____

2 _____

3 _____

4 _____

5 _____

NOVEMBER

_____ 6

_____ 7

_____ 8

_____ 9

_____ 10

NOVEMBER

11 _____

12 _____

13 _____

14 _____

15 _____

NOVEMBER

_____ 16

_____ 17

_____ 18

_____ 19

_____ 20

NOVEMBER

21 _____

22 _____

23 _____

24 _____

25 _____

NOVEMBER

26

27

28

29

30

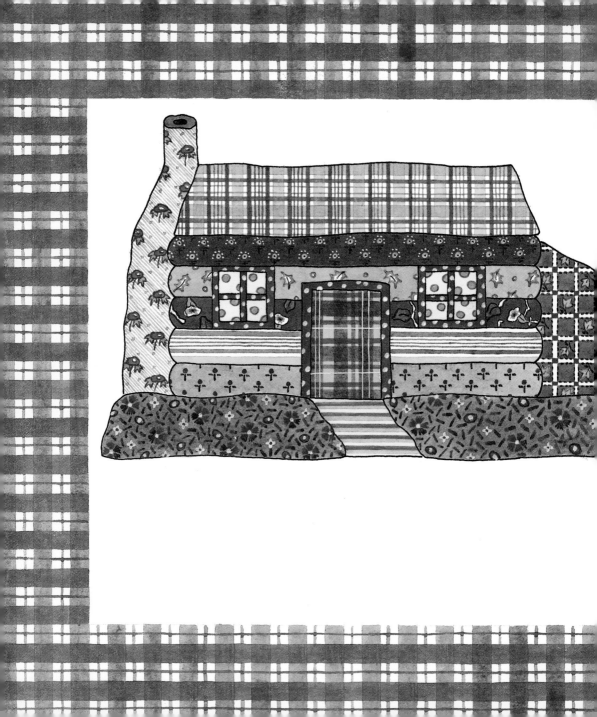

DECEMBER

DECEMBER

1 _____

2 _____

3 _____

4 _____

5 _____

DECEMBER

6

7

8

9

10

DECEMBER

11 _____

12 _____

13 _____

14 _____

15 _____

DECEMBER

16

_____

17

_____

18

_____

19

_____

20

_____

DECEMBER

21 _____

22 _____

23 _____

24 _____

25 _____

DECEMBER

26

27

28

29

30

31

Published in the UK by Museum Quilts (UK) Inc.,
254-258 Goswell Road, London EC1V 7EB

Published in the USA by Sterling Publishing Company, Inc.,
387 Park Avenue South, New York, NY 10016
and by Museum Quilts Publications.
Distributed in Canada by Sterling Publishing
c/o Canadian Manda Group, P.O. Box 920, Station U
Toronto, Ontario, Canada M8Z 5P9.
Distributed in Australia by Capricorn Link (Australia) Pty Ltd.
P.O. Box 6651, Baulkham Hills, Business Centre, NSW 2153, Australia.

Printed and bound in Korea

ISBN: 1 897954 46 8